PIG IN THE AIR

CLIVE SCRUTON

WITH WORDS BY DAVID LLOYD

WALKER BOOKS
LONDON

Who said pigs can't fly?

Watch me try!

I've had an idea.

Come in here!

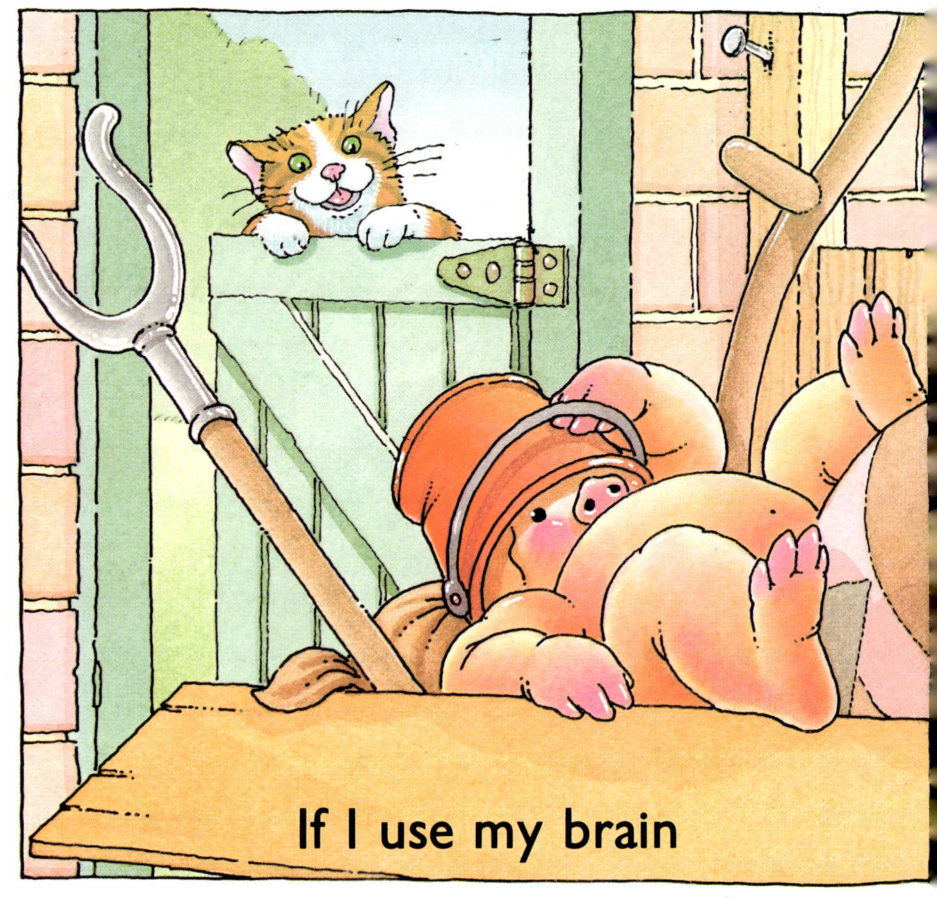

If I use my brain

I can make

On your marks! Get ready!

Get steady!

I'll fly to the moon!

See you soon!

I know! I’ve got it!

I’ll be a rocket!

Up, up and away!

Hip! Hip! Hip!

Watch out down below!

No! No! No!

I flew! I flew!